THE UNIVERSE STORY IN SCIENCE AND MYTH

GreenSpirit book series

THE
Universe Story
in Science and Myth

Greg Morter and Niamh Brennan

Published by GreenSpirit
137 Ham Park Road, London E7 9LE
www.greenspirit.org.uk

Registered Charity No. 1045532

© Greg Morter and Niamh Brennan 2016
First published in the GreenSpirit ebook series in 2013

ISBN 978-0-9935983-8-8

All rights reserved. Except for brief quotations in critical articles or reviews, no part of this book may be reproduced in any manner without prior written permission from the authors.

Design and artwork by Stephen Wollaston (Santoshan)
Printed by CreateSpace and Amazon
Front cover and inside image © Ase/Shutterstock.com

Contents

Introduction   7

In the Beginning   11
Atoms   13
Stars   15
Galaxies   18
Earth   19
Life   22
Photosynthesis   24
Respiration   25
The Complex Cell   26
Multicellularity   28
Global Ice Age   31
Complex Life   33
Landwards   35
Forests and Reptiles   36
Great Continent   38
Dinosaurs   40
Flowering Plants   42
Mammal Time   44
Bipedal Apes   46
Humanity   47
The Evolution of Consciousness   49

One Source	53
Creativity and Imagination	57
Time	62
Death and Destruction	68
Compassion and Justice	74
Beneath the Surface ~ a Call to the Depths	77
Awe	82
Glossary	84
Bibliography: Greg Morter	87
Bibliography: Niamh Brennan	89
About the Authors	91
GreenSpirit Book Series and Other Resources	92

INTRODUCTION

Every being has a story. A time when they came into existence; a time when they were moulded and transformed through circumstance and experience; a time when they begin to age and decay. Cultures, too, have their stories. Many of these we know as myths, as ancient ways of explaining how our world came to be. For the human, story helps us to create meaning and to understand events. Story contextualises. In a world where we have constant and immediate access only to our own thoughts, words and deeds, we need story to locate ourselves within the larger context of life of which we are just a part.

Throughout history each cultural group has had a creation story or myth. This was the story within which they oriented their lives. It acted as a guide by which to navigate through life's uncertainties and difficulties. Using analogy, it sought to explain such phenomenon as human suffering and death. It was a mythical answer to the fundamental existential human questions such as why are we here, do we matter, is there a God? Our creation stories are important because they reflect the beliefs and value systems that a culture holds and in turn help to shape the beliefs and values of individuals. For a long time, much of the Western world has been without an effective creation story. This has led to a disorientation in the human condition, to whole cultures not knowing who they are or where they have come from, to mindless destruction of the ecosystems that sustain us on this planet, our only home, the creation.

A new creation story is needed, one that is both mythical and based on fact, that transcends religion but can incorporate it, that enunciates scientifically but with the vision of the poet, one that speaks to people with the power to awe them back into life. The story being told in this book is that story. It is the story of that which is the ultimate context. It too, has its own story, a story that the people of our times are the first to be able to tell. This is the story of the Universe. It is also the story of Earth, of life, of the human and of the power of conscious thought.

Thomas Berry once wrote how Earth is primary and the human is derivative. By extension it can be said that the Universe is primary and that Earth is derivative. The Universe does not exist 'out there' in space, it is in us, part of us, as we are for our short lives, part of it. But this is knowledge that we are only newly acquiring and it is the people of this century who, with the information from the sciences, can speak for the first time in history about the Universe in which we live. We are now able to know certain things about it, such as how it began, how old it is currently estimated to be, how it evolved and transformed through time, and the structures and dynamics that govern it. We also have greater knowledge of Earth, the part of the Universe that we are most intimate with, that we have direct access to, and the part of the Universe that physically formed us.

The story of the Universe is the epic unfolding of the world, an evolutionary tale of awesome scope. It speaks of unity and diversity, of desire and curiosity, of wonder and awe. It speaks of creativity and imagination, of death, destruction and transformation. It is the story of science. It is the story of spirit. It is the story of all beings, extinct, present and yet to be born. It is a sacred story of magical unfolding, a story that is still being born and told in you and me, now. It is a story, once known, that has the power to inspire our species into becoming the species we were born to be.

* * *

In the Beginning

The Universe flared into existence 13.8 billion years ago. That's 13 800 000 000 or 13.8 thousand million years: an inconceivably huge and incomprehensible timespan. Its appearance is a moment of intense mystery; we cannot say, and perhaps never will be able to say with any certainty, how or why this happened. It is tempting to view the process, in our imaginations, from the outside – as some kind of explosion expanding into space. This is a mistake, because there was no 'outside', no pre-existing space for the Universe to unfurl into. Both space and time emerged with the Universe; they had no existence before it. Our conception of an explosion also implies a single point of origin. But wherever we go in the cosmos, wherever we set up our telescopes to observe the superclusters of galaxies, we will find them racing away from us. The expansion of the Universe is omnicentric; its point of origin is everywhere. Our imaginations are incapable of comprehension; our only sanctuary is our sense of awe.

The emergent fireball was a formless void of incredibly intense temperature and density; but it was expanding and cooling fast. After the tiniest fraction of a second, gravity, electromagnetism and the two other forces that shape our reality, the strong and weak nuclear force, began to unfurl from the chaos. The fireball seethed with photons, miniscule bundles of energy. When two photons collided they destroyed each other, but conjured into being paired particles of matter and antimatter. When these met they were in turn annihilated, in the process creating a photon of light. Each particle collided with another, disappeared and scattered in a new form millions of times in every instant.

This cauldron of creativity and destruction continued until the Universe was a second old, when the temperature had declined to ten billion °C – too cool for photons to collide with sufficient energy to be obliterated. So the creation of new matter/antimatter pairings ceased. As the remainder of these continued to annihilate each other, it transpired that for every billion antimatter particles, a billion and one particles of matter had been created. From this trifling, miraculous asymmetry the substance of our Universe was brought forth.

* * *

Atoms

By the time all the antimatter had disappeared, matter had organised itself into three forms – protons with a positive charge, electrons with a negative charge and neutrons with no charge. After three minutes, temperatures had declined to a billion °C and neutrons and protons were moving sufficiently slowly to begin to be able to form themselves into small atomic nuclei. Seventeen minutes later, when the temperature had dropped below 10 million °C, it was already too cool for them to do this. The vast majority of matter was still in the form of single protons, which are the nuclei of the element hydrogen. About a quarter of the mass had formed helium nuclei, with two protons and two neutrons, while a trace had become heavy hydrogen (with a single proton and neutron) and a couple of heavier elements.

Although the Universe had expanded substantially since the beginning it was still fantastically dense. Photons of light could only travel for a fraction of a second before they interacted with electrons and protons and were scattered or absorbed. We experience a similar phenomenon, albeit at vastly lower temperatures, when it is foggy; light cannot travel freely as it is repeatedly scattered by molecules of water vapour. It took around 380 000 years for this impasse to shift. Electrons have a tiny mass – about two thousandth of that of a neutron or proton – and so all this time they had continued to career around at huge speeds. Now the temperature had fallen to 3000 °C, and they were moving slowly enough to begin to notice the electrical attraction of the protons. All over the Universe the electrons were drawn into relationship with protons, forming atoms of hydrogen and helium. This represented a dramatic shift of scale. From our perspective atoms are tiny – 100 million can line up side by side in each centimetre – but from the perspective of a nucleus they are vast structures, with a radius over 10 000 times as large. There was no intimation that such a revolutionary development was about to happen, but the potential for future creativity was deeply enhanced. Such moments of intense surprise, in which a new reality unexpectedly emerges, will be a recurring theme as the story unfolds.

Atoms are, to a large extent, transparent to light and so for the first time the primeval light from the fireball decoupled itself from matter and moved freely. As it travelled across expanding space its wavelength was gradually stretched. Today this afterglow of the Big Bang appears in the microwave part of the spectrum and is detectable by radio telescopes; it is called the Cosmic Microwave Background (CMB) radiation.

* * *

Stars

After 10 million years the wavelength of the CMB was stretched beyond the visible spectrum and the Universe entered a period known as the Dark Age. But hydrogen and helium were busy organising themselves for a new development. At decoupling they had been very uniformly, but not perfectly, distributed. Where they were slightly more concentrated they were able to gravitationally attract more atoms to themselves and in this way clumps of material gradually formed. By 200 million years these had collected into vast clouds of gas, which began to collapse in on themselves, compressing and heating their centres. When temperatures reached 3000 °C, atoms were stripped of their electrons. But the collapse continued unabated until the core became so dense and hot – with temperatures exceeding 10 million °C – that conditions in the first minutes after the Big bang were recreated. Hydrogen nuclei began to fuse together into helium nuclei, releasing vast amounts of energy. This created an outward radiation pressure which halted the inward collapse of the cloud. A new self-organising structure, the first star, was falteringly finding its equilibrium. Soon, stars were lighting up throughout the Universe; the Dark Age was over.

The Sun is a star, transforming hydrogen to helium in this way and bathing us in the light released by the reaction. All life on Earth is dependent upon it. But what is most critical about stars at this stage in our story is that they are alchemical; they forge new elements that have not existed before. The first stars were 200 times the mass of our Sun and their lives were short and tempestuous. A star of this size can attain such fantastic temperatures that it only takes a few million years to use up all the hydrogen in the core. Without radiation pressure to hold it up, the core then collapses, heating to 100 million °C. At this temperature helium fuses into carbon, releasing energy to restabilise the star. This process of core collapse and restabilisation then repeats itself in a series of steps, fusing through successive elements such as oxygen, nitrogen and silicon. Each stage happens at a higher temperature and a faster rate until, once silicon begins to fuse into iron, the star only has a few days before its reserves are exhausted.

At this point the star reaches an impasse because iron nuclei need an input of energy to be able to fuse together. So as the core contracts there is no new radiation pressure to resist it; the iron nuclei are crushed into their constituent parts. Then, as the gravitational pressure intensifies, electrons are forced to combine with protons, forming neutrons and creating a shockwave that rebounds out through the star. The collapse continues, until the core becomes a black hole, a region of space so dense that not even light can escape. After millions of years of existence the star has obliterated itself in a little less than ten seconds.

As the shockwave moves out through the outer shell of the star, at four thousand miles per second, it piles up material in front of itself and pushes up temperatures to around 100 billion °C. In such a furnace atoms heavier than iron can be formed; copper and zinc, gold and silver, mercury, lead, uranium and dozens of other new elements burst into existence. As the star annihilates itself in a supernova explosion, a two-week flash of brilliance as bright as 200 billion suns, they are flung out into the Cosmos. The most appalling destruction has brought forth the basis for wonderful new creativity.

* * *

Galaxies

The element-rich material from the first stars formed vast dust clouds, parts of which collapsed into a second generation of stars. Meanwhile the stars themselves were being swept by gravity into larger and larger conglomerations and by 380 million years the first galaxies had formed. Modern galaxies have typically 200 billion stars, but in their youth they were much smaller and less bright. The black holes, formed in the death throes of the first stars and from supernova explosions of later large stars, began to coagulate at the centre of galaxies. These steadily drew material into themselves, until by two billion years a typical galaxy had a central black hole as massive as a thousand million Suns. Material spiralling into them, at speeds approaching three-quarters of the speed of light, became so hot and compressed that it began to emit X-ray radiation. Galaxies in this turbulent adolescent phase of their evolution are known as quasars and were 1000 times brighter than today. Each galaxy stayed in the quasar stage for about 100 million years before embarking on a more serene middle age. By four billion years quasars had become rare because all the matter in the universe had been swept into galaxies, and all the material close enough to their black holes to spiral in, had done so.

* * *

Earth

A little over four-and-a-half billion years ago, 9.25 billion years after the Universe flared forth, a vast dust cloud floated in a spiral arm, two-thirds of the way out from the centre of the Milky Way galaxy. A gravitational impulse, perhaps from a supernova explosion, set the cloud spinning, causing it to break up into separate fragments. Each of these fragments then began to collapse under its own gravity. As it contracted it spun faster, drawing most material to the centre and pushing out the rest into a swirling disc. Within fifty million years planets had begun to coalesce in these spinning wheels of debris and a star had ignited at their centres. One of these planetary formations was our Solar System. The others, perhaps numbering dozens, containing sister stars to our Sun, have gradually drifted off to other parts of the galaxy. Sadly we are unable to identify them.

The third planet out from the Sun was a rocky, molten infant, buffeted by ceaseless impacts with meteorites, called Earth. It incorporated the material from these collisions into its bulk; the heavier elements, such as iron, sinking to the centre and the lighter forming the crust. As the Earth neared its current size and was beginning to stabilise, it collided with a Mars-sized planet which ploughed into its outer surface. Crustal material from both planets was flung into orbit, while the cores gradually combined at the centre of the Earth.

This catastrophe was a deeply significant moment for the

future creativity of Earth. The orbiting debris, little by little, formed itself into our unusually large Moon, which has both tamed the Earth's wobble and slowed its rotation from four to twenty four hours; creating a stable environment in which evolution could occur. The Earth's large core means it has a particularly large magnetic field protecting water from being split by cosmic rays and its hydrogen lost to space. The collision also tilted Earth's axis, originating the seasons, and initiated volcanic activity which began to build the atmosphere. But the atmosphere was about to receive an even more significant bounty from changes occurring in the outer reaches of the Solar system.

During the last fifty million years the gaseous giants – Jupiter, Saturn, Uranus and Neptune – had gradually taken form. As they grew, their gravitational impact increased until it began to disrupt the integrity of the Oort cloud, a spherical halo of comets at the very edge of the Solar System. From about four-and-a-half billion years ago comets began to be dislodged, hurtling towards the Sun and inner planets. This cometary bombardment lasted for the best part of a billion years, with its greatest intensity in the first half of the period. Comets are essentially large, dirty snowballs. Those that collided with the Earth brought most of its water, carbon and atmospheric gases and all the mineable precious metals; a sustained, hard earned, gift of inestimable value.

Four billion years ago the cometary bombardment was beginning to decline and the Earth was stabilising into something like its current form, with a large iron core, a semi-liquid mantle and a solidifying crust. The atmosphere was scores of times thicker than today, composed mainly of carbon dioxide but also containing nitrogen, methane, carbon monoxide and water vapour. There was no oxygen and it was too hot for liquid water. Over the next couple of hundred million years it continued to cool, until slowly the water vapour began to condense and it started to rain. The first drops turned to steam as they touched the hot crust, but as the rains got into their stride the inhospitable surface was quenched. For millions of years, torrential rain continued unceasingly; seas and then oceans began to form.

* * *

LIFE

The Earth is misleadingly named. 'Sea' would be more accurate; even today two-thirds of the surface is covered in water. In the beginning, when the first rains had done their work, there was almost nothing but ocean. However, land began to be formed in two ways. Above the surface of the water, rain washed carbon dioxide out of the atmosphere to form a weak carbonic acid. It combined with calcium, dissolved in the oceans, and was deposited as the first limestone. Meanwhile, below the surface, ferocious volcanic unrest powered by the supernova-charged radioactivity of the mantle, was beginning to push the odd island into view.

Where exposed mantle met seawater a dramatic chemical reaction took place which caused the rock to rapidly expand and crack. This allowed more seawater to seep in, perpetuating the process and forming a new and exotic structure: an alkaline hydrothermal vent, not to be confused with the more familiar acidic vents, the volcanic black smokers. These formations were only discovered in the year 2000, although their existence was predicted much earlier. They are white, towering up to sixty metres in height, and are permeated with a labyrinth of interlinked microscopic pores. These pores, exactly the size of bacterial cells, are lined with elements such as iron and sulphur, powerful catalysts for chemical reactions. Hydrogen and other gases bubble up through them. When these combine with the carbon dioxide dissolved in seawater they produce organic molecules, and release energy, mimicking a metabolic process found in ancient strains of bacteria. Moreover the reaction between the alkalinity of the vents and the acidity of the oceans creates an energy gradient to get the reactions going. Alkaline vents, it seems, are likely hatcheries for the emergence of life 3.8 billion years ago.

The appearance of life was preceded by chemical evolution. The gases bubbling through the vents contain the elemental diversity to create both amino acids and nucleic acids. Computer simulations suggest that these would have formed spontaneously into proteins and DNA respectively. Eventually a rich and complex metabolism had developed within the pores, powered by a selection pressure favouring those pores most efficiently manufacturing their own raw materials. In a very real sense life had now appeared, but without the formation of a membrane it was tied to its birthplace.

It is thought that two distinct lineages broke free from these rocky roots: the Bacteria are familiar to us all, the Archaea, colonisers of extreme environments such as hot springs and high-saline pools, perhaps less so. Both use DNA as the language of the cell and read it off to make proteins using broadly similar metabolic pathways and enzymes. Extraordinarily, this suggests that they originated in the very same hydrothermal mound. However the enzymes they use to replicate DNA are totally distinct and the structure of their cell walls and membranes is very different. This indicates that they came up with independent means to break free.

* * *

Photosynthesis

Both initially survived by fermenting the abundant nutrients in the early oceans. After a few hundred million years those nutrients started to become scarce and so selection pressure increased for the emergence of a new pathway. The solution was photosynthesis, catching energy from light to construct sugars from water and carbon dioxide. It was invented by a new type of bacteria, the cyanobacteria, which quickly became a significant new lineage. The process releases oxygen, which initially reacted with iron dissolved in the ocean, creating bands of oxidised iron deposits from which we mine the mineral today.

Three and a half billion years ago bacteria began to behave co-operatively forming themselves into stromatolites, pillow-like mounds scattered along the shoreline. On the surface of these, the cyanobacteria busily photosynthesised, while below the fermenters harvested the reactants they produced. Wind-blown sand accreted to the sticky exterior and became embedded in the structure as a new generation of bacteria repopulated the surface. In this way stromatolites gradually enlarged, becoming the first visible structure to appear in the history of life. Some became impressively substantial, towering up to one hundred metres in height. They have been extraordinarily successful, evident in the fossil record petty much ever since, and hanging on even today in bays where high salinity discourages grazers.

* * *

Respiration

As the iron dissolved in the oceans gradually became oxidised, the oxygen level began to build up in the water itself and even to bubble out into the atmosphere. This created a challenge for bacteria as oxygen is very reactive and can quickly kill a cell. By 2.4 billion years ago the amount of oxygen in the water had reached unprecedented levels. Many commentators have imagined this causing a bacterial holocaust; at the very least there was selective pressure for a new lifeway to emerge. That lifeway was respiration, the use of oxygen for the controlled burning of sugars, invented by a new lineage of bacteria, the Breathers. They found themselves with a fantastic advantage, as respiration frees ten times the energy that photosynthesis can. They developed a strong rotary tail, the flagellum, to propel themselves about in the quest for food; some even invented the means to drill into other bacteria for their sustenance. They thrived in the newly oxygenated oceans.

* * *

The Complex Cell

Protons, you may recall, are the positively charged nuclei of hydrogen atoms. When they have different concentrations on the two sides of the membrane of a cell, an electrical field is created. The first organisms developed amazing enzymes, tiny nano-scale machines, to generate and tap energy from this field. One enzyme, which stores the energy in a chemical battery called ATP, is like a rotating motor powered by the inward flow of protons; another has a piston for pumping protons outwards. The electrical field they maintain operates over a tiny distance, only a few millionths of a millimetre, but it has the same voltage as a bolt of lightning and has to be handled with great care. Consequently the cell's genes must be located very close to the membrane so they can quickly create new copies of enzymes as the need arises. This is easy for the Bacteria which are very small, but it means that it is impossible for them to directly evolve into a large and complex organism like a tree or a human being.

Two billion years ago probably the most significant event in the history of life occurred when the Archaea and Bacteria joined forces. It is not clear what led up to this. Perhaps an Archaea had developed the ability to engulf prey and then absorb them through its membrane; or maybe a Breather had drilled into the Archaea to digest it from within. But, regardless of which was predator and which prey, on just one occasion the process ended differently; not with digestion and death, but with collaboration. The Breather remained inside the Archaea, aerobically digesting sugars and tapping energy for its host from the force field around the membrane. This serendipitous alliance broke the energy impasse faced by the bacteria and forged a new organism brimming over with promise, the Complex Cell.

The Breather gradually evolved into the mitochondrion, the powerhouse of all complex cells. Its initial 3000 genes have been pared down to a mere 40 or so, those essential for respiration and the maintenance of the proton electrical field. Its presence as a genetic outpost near the membrane gifted its host the ability – and the surplus energy – to steadily enlarge its size and its genome, which it centralised within the protective embrace of the nucleus. That first Complex Cell is the common ancestor of all animals and fungi. With the acquisition of cyanobacteria, which evolved into chloroplasts – the tiny structures in each plant cell undertaking photosynthesis – it also sired the whole of the plant kingdom. The cells of all complex organisms contain hundreds of mitochondria; their lives would be impossible, they would literally have no energy, without them. On that tender thread of fate that brought the mitochondrion and its host together hangs all the wondrous complexity that surrounds us.

* * *

Multicellularity

Whereas the emergence of the complex cell was a one-off improbable event, the transition to multicellularity was seemingly fairly easy, having been achieved independently in plants, animals and fungi. Plants were very quick off the mark; some fossils of *Grypania*, a curled up spiral about a centimetre in diameter, are two billion years old. However for the next one thousand million years – a period dubbed by biologists the "Boring Billion" – very little changed, and it took even longer than this for the first tiny multicellular animals to appear. It is not clear why; perhaps oxygen levels were too low for large life forms. Indeed there is evidence that for much of this time the oceans were polluted with hydrogen sulphide – sewer gas – turning them noxious and stagnant.

The first animal to become multicellular, and thus the ancestor of us all, was something like a modern sponge. The first stage in the process was the formation of a colony of single-celled organisms, possibly as a protective response to the presence of a toxin, such as oxygen, in the water. It would then have been advantageous for the colony to develop some form of chemical communication between its constituent cells, for example to harmonise the movement of tails so it could swim more efficiently. If the colony stayed together eventually cells would have begun to differentiate; some would have specialised in locomotion, others in producing glue to stick the colony to rocks, still others in filtering food particles from the water. Eventually specialised cells for reproduction emerged; each generation then produced genetically unique individuals, variously endowed in their ability to harness resources. Natural selection, the process of filtering out those less suited to their environment, was greatly accelerated and enhanced.

It is poignant to note that the gradual emergence of the wonders of multicellular life, also unleashed natural death. Although bacteria can be killed they do not have a lifespan; it is even possible that some individuals, spawned from the very first generation to escape the hydrothermal vents, still cling on in some recess of the oceans. In contrast, for complex creatures death is an inevitable companion. Programmed cell death is intrinsic to the unfolding of the embryo and the maintenance of organs; while cellular respiration slowly undermines the vitality and effective functioning of large organisms, unavoidably heralding their demise. But in this way nature creates a space to unfurl even greater creativity. As Goethe succinctly observed, "Life is nature's most exquisite invention; and death is her expert contrivance to get plenty of life."

Earth is now on the cusp of dramatic change. As we whirl through a gallery of novel plants and animals it will be easy to lose sight of the bacteria and the other microscopic organisms that helped to build the theatre and set the stage. Of course they are still with us, an intrinsic and vital part of all organisms and ecosystems, and an essential component in their healthy functioning. It is also important to remember that the theatre and stage are under a constant process of redesign and adaption. Earth is not a static backdrop for the evolution of plants and animals; rather the atmosphere, rocks and biosphere together enact an exquisitely intricate dance of holistic evolution.

* * *

Global Ice Age

When it rains, carbon dioxide in the air is incorporated into raindrops as carbonic acid. This weak acid erodes rocks, combining with the silicates they contain to form carbonates; hence carbon dioxide is drawn down from the atmosphere. When, around 850 million years ago, the continents began to form themselves into a band around the equator, this process was accelerated by the severity of tropical storms. The ratio of atmospheric carbon dioxide declined to such an extent that global temperatures began to fall; ice appeared at the poles. Whereas water absorbs 90% of sunlight, ice reflects 85% of it back to space. So the ice sheets gradually began to expand and as their expansion was over water – all the land was further south – the drawdown of carbon continued apace. Global temperatures continued to decline and the ice sheets continued to expand until eventually their expansion became unstoppable. The Earth was plunged into an intense period of glaciation, when average temperatures fell to an excoriating -30°C and the whole globe became covered with ice. Life barely survived, clinging on around warm vents and where the ice was thin and clear.

For millions of years volcanic eruptions punched their way through the ice. There was no rain – it was too cold for water to evaporate – so the level of carbon dioxide began to build again. When it constituted 10% of the atmosphere, the ice began to melt, slowly at first and then catastrophically fast.

Under that warm blanket of carbon dioxide temperatures soared to 50°C and the weather shifted into a cycle of appalling violence; intense hurricanes, million year rainstorms and 100-metre tsunamis convulsed the globe. Carbon, rapidly drawn down from the atmosphere, turned the oceans into an acid bath, before precipitating into bands of carbonate rock at times hundreds of metres thick. Then the inflow of nutrients caused by the tumultuous weathering created the biggest algal bloom in history.

After tens of millions of years, carbon dioxide in the atmosphere was reduced to a level where the whole cycle began again; the Earth suffered perhaps four such periods of global glaciation, followed by the extreme temperatures of a Hothouse, before the continents rearranged themselves enough to prevent it. The algal blooms following the intense erosion of the Hothouses locked up vast quantities of carbon and released free oxygen into the atmosphere. By the end of the Snowball era levels of oxygen were nearing current levels and the scene was set for dramatic change

* * *

Complex Life

The first multicellular ecosystem, the Ediacaran, emerged 590 million years ago. It was dominated by large inactive animals that we would not recognise as kin; animals only in the sense that they lacked chloroplasts, for they also lacked limbs, internal organs and animal senses. Platter-like, firmly attached to the sea floor and untroubled by predators they basked in the Precambrian sun, filter feeding or hosting photosynthetic bacteria. Stromatolites flourished alongside them. Our ancestor, resembling a tiny jellyfish, floated near the surface of the water passively harvesting plankton. During the next 45 million years it transformed itself into a fish-like shape with a through-gut and a specialised front end – with a mouth, a rudimentary brain and a light sensitive patch. Around 545 million years ago it began to use its sucker-like mouth to burrow into the sea floor and graze the platter-beasts, who had no defence against such an assault. The whole ecosystem rapidly collapsed.

The use of the mouth in this way heralds the start of the Cambrian explosion, when a new competitive dynamic between predator and prey began, and a huge diversity of fossilisable creatures appeared. The first innovation was the ability to secrete protective shells. Within twenty million years horrendous mouth parts and pincers had emerged, and many creatures had become much larger. Many groups now familiar to us, such as crabs and bivalves, had evolved, alongside an equal number of more exotic forms. The most ferocious of these was *Anomolocaris*, a metre long predator with spiny leading pincers; the most numerous were the trilobites, like giant, heavily-armoured, marine woodlice, seeking out prey with their compound crystal eyes. Coral was first laid down at this time; although it is formed by different creatures at different times, it will now be a consistently present feature.

* * *

Landwards

By 450 million years ago both the backbone and a simple jaw had evolved on our ancestral line. Huge armour-plated fish called placoderms patrolled the seas searching for prey. Their armour protected them from eurypterids, giant sea scorpions, which lurked in the mud ready to pounce on unsuspecting passing victims. Animals and plants fled this onslaught into the relative safety of freshwater rivers and lakes; and from there they began to colonise the land.

The first colonisers were the plants, initially clinging low on the water's edge, but becoming more substantial as they gradually learned to stay wet on the inside while being dry on the outside. They teamed up with fungi in an elegant symbiosis in which plants had their root systems extended in return for excess sugars. Tiny crustaceans, spiders and wingless insects came ashore and began to scuttle about. Soil, composed of weathered rock and the dead residue of all this activity, started to accumulate.

The lungfish probably evolved when, returning to the sea after spawning in the headwaters of a river, they had to haul themselves through dried up riverbed. As their terrestrial surroundings became more lush they began to linger there, tempted by the abundance of food. Gradually some evolved into amphibians, spending their adult life on land and their larval stage in water.

* * *

Forests and Reptiles

Around 420 million years ago the plants invented wood, which allowed them to grow larger and develop internal plumbing for transporting water and nutrients. By the start of the Carboniferous period, 359 million years ago, forests, of fern, club moss and horsetail trees, clothed the land; although its participants have changed, the forest ecosystem has been with us ever since. Swamp forests, in which much of our coal was created, were at this time the dominant form, but plants were learning to become fully terrestrial. Some had already developed seeds which, unlike spores, are able to withstand periods of drought. By the end of the period conifers emerged. So much carbon was tied up in wood and coal that the oxygen level rose to about 35% (compared to 21% today), allowing insects to grow huge. Dragonflies, the first winged insects, fluttered through the trees, some as big as seagulls. Human-sized millipedes, the largest 2 1/2 metres in length, giant spiders and 70 cm long scorpions scuttled around in the undergrowth.

Amphibians were the dominant animal group during the Carboniferous, varying from as small as a newt to several metres in size. Like plants, they also experienced selection pressure to live purely on land. The development of shelled, internally-fertilised eggs that did not dry out in air occurred in the group that became the reptiles. With both their reproductive cycle and their young liberated from water they were able to begin to explore the vast potential of the continental interiors. Mammals have reptilian origins and although our ancestor quickly split off from them, the reptilian instincts for survival, sustenance and sex were already deeply embedded in our make-up.

* * *

Great Continent

From 300 million years ago the continents began to form themselves into one large land mass, dubbed Pangaea, stretching across the equator from pole to pole. A vast central area of desert was, in favourable areas, interspersed with the occasional relict of carboniferous forest, though this was increasingly outcompeted by an ecosystem based around conifers. An immense ice sheet on the South Pole was fringed by extensive groves of the willow-leaved tree *Glossopteris*, while along river banks the gingko tree made its first appearance. The first complex food chain emerged, dominated by thirty to forty of our ancestors, the mammal-like reptiles. Lizard-like herbivores, some as big as hippos roamed around in herds while lizard-like insectivores snuffled in the undergrowth. These were preyed upon by *Dimetrodon*, their large sail allowing them to be active much earlier in the morning and the *gorgonopsian*, an ugly ten feet long amalgam of a lion and a lizard. The predators benefitted from significant improvements in the musculature of the jaw, facilitating chewing and clamping.

Around 250 million years ago a mass extinction occurred, in which much of this diversity disappeared. Between half and three-quarters of all land species and 95% of all marine species became extinct. For the first time in history even the insects took a severe knock. The catastrophe happened in a number of pulses. The supercontinent itself caused the first of these, bringing together in competition lineages from different land masses. Perhaps more importantly its formation minimised sea-shelf, one of the most diverse of habitats. So ecosystems were already under pressure when a supervolcano in Siberia became active. It continued to erupt for half a million years, covering an area the size of the Europe in a kilometre depth of lava, causing acid rain and pumping out enough carbon dioxide to raise global temperatures. Ice at the poles began to melt, releasing methane (another greenhouse gas) trapped below the permafrost, which further cranked up the thermostat.

When temperatures had risen to 6°C above pre-volcanic levels, the forest eco-system collapsed. Debris poured into the seas, which became stagnant and sterile. In the absence of predators, stromatolites returned to the global stage; and fungi, nature's recyclers, experienced a significant spike. No coal is found in the geological record for six million years and no coral for over twenty million years. At least ten million years passed before plants were able to recover the habit of being trees.

* * *

Dinosaurs

Our only ancestor to survive the devastation was *Lystrosaurus*, resembling a squat, short tailed, burrowing, lizard-featured housecat. During the early Triassic it rapidly occupied vacant niches, evolving into both three metre long herbivores and their ferocious predators. On the reptilian line, snakes, crocodiles and lizards emerged, pterosaurs took to the sky, and ichthyosaurs ventured into the oceans. Then, around 230 million years ago a reptile evolved with its legs directly under the body. It was so successful that it founded a new dynasty: the dinosaurs.

Dinosaurs dominated the world for the next 165 million years. They spread to all continents, occupied all niches, and varied in size from about the dimensions of a modern pigeon to the sixty metre long sauropods, which could with ease reach in to eat the cut flowers on your attic bedroom window sill. Dinosaurs were not, as often depicted, slow and stupid, but fast, agile and alert. Beneath their gaze the first mammals emerged about 210 million years ago, to begin their long career as small, nocturnal, shrew-like animals cowering in the undergrowth.

Early mammals almost certainly shared many attributes of our modern mammalian cousins, the monotremes (the duck-billed platypus is the most well-known example). Monotreme means 'single hole' and, in common with modern birds and reptiles, the first mammals would have used the same orifice to urinate, defecate and reproduce. Monotremes lay eggs and secrete milk for their young from modified sweat glands on a wide area of skin on the front of their torso. They also have sprawling reptilian limbs. Early mammals would have shared these traits.

During the Jurassic (from 200 to 145 million years ago) the Dinosaurs continued to dominate; towards the end they also sired a new lineage – the birds. It is an extraordinary thought that the descendants of dinosaurs unobtrusively hop and fly through our gardens. Around 180 million years ago the monotremes split from the other mammals, the latter subsequently producing modern mammalian characteristics such as warm blood, hair, extended parental care, and basic social instincts including a sense of status and the experience of rejection. The exact timing of the emergence of such qualities is difficult to ascertain, however, as they leave few clues in the fossil record.

The creatures that star in the film 'Jurassic Park' actually lived in the following period, the Cretaceous. *Tyrannosaurus rex*, for example, is found in the fossil record between 67 and 65.5 million years ago; it is sobering to note that this is much closer in time to us than to its own ancestors in the mid-Triassic. During the Cretaceous, beneath deep subtropical seas, thick seams of chalk were laid down by accumulated corpses of tiny algae known as coccoliths, a thousand of which could fit on a pinhead. Early in the period the placentals, the group to which we belong, split from the marsupials which continued to thrive and diversify in Australasia and South America.

* * *

Flowering Plants

About 120 million years ago, after 4.5 billion years of development, the Earth burst into flower. This extraordinary moment not only brought forth new beauty, but also laid the basis for our own emergence. For if we went back in time before the first flowers we would find little that would be palatable for us to eat; fish and some of the early birds may have been tasty but beyond that we would find only pine nuts, unless we decided to risk some unfamiliar leaves or mushrooms. The vast majority of what we eat today is either a flowering plant or a species that depends on them. Some of the first flowers, which resembled magnolias, gradually evolved large nutritious fruit and nuts; others pared down their structure to become wind pollinated grasses, which later sustained generations of herbivores and which we recently domesticated into wheat, rice and maize.

Seventy million years ago, tempted by the cornucopia emerging in the flowering trees, our ancestor ventured into their boughs. There it became a primate, its body and senses sculpted anew by the distinct selection pressures of this novel environment. Forward facing binocular eyes were essential for judging the distance to the next branch. The need to distinguish ripe from unripe fruit necessitated the development of good (trichromatic) colour vision, while the sense of smell, which had been so essential on the ground, tended to atrophy. Grasping hands and feet, good shoulder mobility, and opposable thumbs all became essential qualities.

Sixty five million years ago a ten mile wide asteroid, travelling at 60 000 miles per hour, thudded into the coast of Mexico. It blasted out a crater 120 miles wide, initiating a seismic report and wind-shock that reverberated around the globe. Ecosystems were devastated by global forest fires and pulverised by 150 metre tsunamis. Smoke, dust and ash blotted out the sun, instituting a 3-year perpetual night. All creatures over 55lbs, including the dinosaurs, pterosaurs and ichthyosaurs, were wiped out. The survivors, probably deaf and blind, reduced to scavenging, barely managed to raise their young.

* * *

Mammal Time

The new generation that did emerge found themselves, in the absence of the dinosaurs, in a world full of opportunity. Fish, mammals, birds, flowering plants and insects all embarked on a period of bewildering diversification. Within 3 million years our shrew-like ancestors had dog-sized companions. They were initially preyed on by giant birds and crocodiles; two million years later they also had to reckon with the first mammal carnivores. When, fifty million years ago average global temperatures peaked at an incredible 28°C, and then began their long steady decline to the present, the warm blooded mammals gradually started to experience a competitive advantage; as the poles steadily cooled and the continental centres dried out, they became larger, faster and more dominant.

Forty million years ago the first anthropoid – a group including monkeys, apes and humans – appears in the fossil record. It was a tiny (4oz) tree dweller. Thirty million years ago the apes split off from the monkeys, losing their tails in the process. Five million years later, grassland became a significant ecosystem in the drying continental interiors. Grass is unique in that it grows from the base and so is very tolerant of, indeed thrives on, grazing; so herds of herbivores evolved in tandem with the grassland. By twenty million years ago, although it was still warmer than today, the climate and vegetation would be recognisable to us; all modern mammal groups were present and our ancestor split from the gibbons. Fourteen million years ago, when it was cool enough for ice to form at the poles, she split from the orangutans. Four million years later she split from the gorillas.

* * *

Bipedal Apes

Six million years ago our common ancestor with the chimpanzees lived in the forests of east Africa, eating berries, nuts and leaves. One day a small group left the safety of the trees and ventured into the savannah. They stumbled across a carcass, left over from the previous night's carnivore hunt, and into a new lifeway. By 4.2 million years ago they had evolved into the Australopithecines, a bipedal apelike hominid, living permanently in this fringe between wood and grassland, supplementing their plant based diet with scavenged meat. Excellent climbers they were able to quickly clamber up trees to safety when the need arose.

A new group, Homo habilis, emerged 2.4 million years ago. Their thick, long thumbs and fingers and wide hands gave them a precision grip, with which they began to use tools; sharp flakes chipped from cobbles helped to skin and dismember meat, while the cobble core was used to club bones to extract the marrow.

Homo erectus knapped more elegant bifacial tools. Emerging 1.8 million years ago, they were tall, slim and hairless; a physique adapted to run down and exhaust game on the savannah. They were the first hominids to explore other continents, some migrating to Asia – where they probably tamed fire and where they survived until about 30 000 years ago.

* * *

Humanity

Our ancestors remained in Africa. By 500 000 years ago they were hafting stone blades to wooden hunting spears and using fire to cook. One group moved north, adapting to hunt big game in the frozen chill of Ice Age Europe: the Neanderthals. A second group remained behind and by 200 000 had developed a sharp edged and standardised toolkit, honed with great skill and craftsmanship. Even more significantly they had begun to use language. They were Homo sapiens: modern humans.

About 80 000 years ago a group of maybe 200 moderns left Africa and set off around the south coast of Arabia. Their descendants spread out into Asia, then made the 40 miles sea crossing into Australia as early as 65 000 years ago. They began to colonise Europe 40 000 years ago and crossed the frozen Bering Strait into America 25 000 later. All this time their technologies were improving; around 60 000 years ago bows and arrows were first used, while cave painting, sculpture and musical instruments became common 35 000 years ago. At the same time, migration into the cooler north prompted the invention of the needle and tailored clothing.

In the warm, wet climate that followed the retreat of the glaciers, from 18 000 years ago onwards, the abundance of food, in areas such as the Nile Valley and the Fertile Crescent in the Near East, allowed people to become more sedentary and populations to increase. A subsequent cool snap forced an intensification of food production, and 11 000 years ago settled agricultural villages began to appear. Within 6000 years many of these villages were being swept into the orbit of cities and then into states; complex power structures, war and writing had emerged and together they began to sculpt the radical transformations that led to the modern era.

* * *

The Evolution of Consciousness

This extraordinary six million year journey from forest to city engendered, and in turn was facilitated by, a profound shift in consciousness. The early hominids were embedded in a timeless nature, seamlessly at one with their environment. Perhaps half a million years ago a dim self-awareness began to emerge, a glimmer of awakening to an embodied self in a passing present. This sense became more concrete with the appearance of language, with its possibility of symbolism and its evocation of a remembered past and an imagined future. A similar consciousness is experienced today by members of relict hunter-gather groups who have a sense of individual identity but commonly experience themselves flowing in and out of others and of nature.

Agriculture embedded us in a sense of cyclic time, but also demanded that we separate ourselves and observe how nature works. Emergent crafts required similar analysis but engendered a different relationship to time ("How long will it take to fire this pot?"). Cities made us even more remote from nature, and developed deeper abstractions such as accounting and writing.

All cultures experienced this separation from nature as a wrench. Almost all cultures have a story of the 'Fall' from this oneness with nature, experienced and expressed as a break with

Divinity. By the time of the Axial Age (800-200 BCE) many people, particularly in cities, experienced the Divine as remote and difficult to access; how to respond to this loss became a significant preoccupation. The answer, from China and India across to Europe, was a new emphasis on compassion, justice and individual morality, and a deep exploration of the relationship between myth and rationality. This moment is commonly seen as marking the arrival of the modern human.

But change is constant. If we went back in time 500 years we would find ways of speech, gender relations, hierarchies of power and the possibilities for making a living very alien to us. But what would astound and trouble us most would be the ways of thinking; about what is known, what can be known, and our place in the Universe. We tend to see our own way of thinking as somehow 'natural', but even thought has a history and our minds are a product of that history. The modern mind has been deeply sculpted by the scientific and philosophical revolution of the past 500 years; it will continue to be sculpted by new revelations and ways of seeing.

* * *

This is the story we have learned from science. It is the facts gained through empirical observation and experiment. But what is the meaning of this story? What might we, a humanity who struggles with our place and our role in this vast Universe, take it to mean?

Whilst there are many things that we do not know about the Universe in which we live, there are also many things that we do know. We do know that this Universe is a journey began some 13.8 billion years ago; we do know that the Universe continues to expand and that most of what it is composed of is called dark matter. We do know how our solar system and within it, our own planet was formed. We know how life has evolved through the millennia and how deeply interconnected and interdependent the process of life is.

These discoveries demand that we re-envision our sense of self and that we re-think what it means to be human in light of the knowledge that we are now privileged to be learning about the Universe in which we live. The information is challenging but just as the Universe expands, so too can our minds expand and with them, maybe even our hearts. It is no longer viable to see the world as static and unchanging, as inanimate and mechanical. The whole world is telling this ancient story, each being in its own inimitable way. As the human element, we too, tell this story. With this new knowledge, we can be informed about how best to tell it, about the choices we make, the qualities we value and the kind of future we wish to create.

Science tells us that there are qualities that we can associate with the Universe, qualities that are intrinsic to it and it's unfolding, a quality being such that it allows us to make a statement about the Universe which we regard as true. Such a statement might be – it is a creative Universe; it is a differentiated Universe; it is a just or a compassionate Universe. What we can say about the Universe is important because it holds lessons for us, its human manifestation. We do not stand outside of it but rather are part of its becoming. If there are pervasive Universal qualities, then what can we, must we, learn from these qualities?

This 'new story' can provide us with a fresh pair of eyes with which to gaze upon the world, it can provide us with a mind that is softened and more opened to the world's wonder and mystery, with a heart that is thoughtful and reflective of where it came from. It can provide us with guidance as we work our way into a future where all species are equally valued, where Earth is treated as a gift and not a commodity and where life is a hope-filled adventure of ever more discovery.

* * *

One Source

Science is a description of the physical, chemical and biological layers that drive our world. It examines the world and its processes and seeks through theory and experiment to explain them. Science has given us the gift of this story. It tells how the Universe has developed through time and how, starting from a point the size of a pinprick, it has transformed from energy to atoms, to stars, to galaxies, to Earth. Science also tells us that everything that ever was and that will ever be, was contained in that fireball which burst into existence so splendidly and so mysteriously some 13.8 billion years ago. The origin of all things from one source. A source whose existence itself is inexplicable, shrouded in a mystery that the human has not yet been able to penetrate. A source that is becoming physically more expressed as time passes, making explicit that which has been implicit since the beginning.

So what is the significance of coming from the same source? It means that connection and relationship are fundamental to our existence. Not only do we have a common ancestor but we have a shared beginning making us different expressions of the same thing, making us One. Think of the seed of the pansy, planted in early spring that begins to bloom in summer, its slight, green stem and leaves complimented by an assortment of flowers of white, purple and yellow, each expressing something specific of the nature of the pansy but all coming from the same seed, all the one plant. So it is with this Universe, it takes its expression in different forms. The Universe in the form of a galaxy: the Universe in the form of Earth: the Universe in the form of you. A common energy travelling through time expressing itself differently but equally present in each form. This ancient source, that Jean Gebser named the Ever Present Origin is the energy that permeates the world and all its beings, connecting us all, as present in others as it is in me, as sacred in others as it is in me.

For many centuries, the concepts of separation, isolation and aloneness have occupied the thoughts of our post-industrialist mind. The more we have developed our thinking, the more we have been able to objectify ourselves and to think of ourselves as separate beings. This has created a sense of loneliness which now seems part of the human condition. And yet this new information from science is telling us that separation is an illusion, as is isolation, so why do we indulge them? We are all, in a particular form, a result of that initial flaring forth, sharing that same energy, that same divine spark of life. We share, and are part of, one physical body. We all breathe the same air, drink the same water, walk on the same Earth. We enter the world through the body of another being, share the same genes and DNA with others; share the same molecules and atoms which when we die are released back into the biosphere again to be recycled into other beings. There is not a single being that could exist alone or in isolation. It defies creation. It defies science. We are interdependent and connected out of necessity. No being can do all things. We need others to fill the gaps, such is the way the Universe creates.

So why do we feel alone? I can only think at the moment that it is because we do not know who we are. We stunt ourselves with our classifications of gender, race and class, differences that are mostly superficial and which ignore this common 14 billion year energy that is burning in all of us. We fetter ourselves when we create divisions of land, boundaries that are only human made – as if this four billion year old world and all that it took to create it, could possibly be 'owned' or possessed by a newly arrived and entirely dependent species. I wonder what does that tell us about our sense of self that we imagine we can buy and sell the very entity that brought us forth?

We delude ourselves when we act from the belief that superiority of being, of intelligence, of ethic, lies in the colour of the outward layer of skin that covers our body and fool ourselves even further when we think that only institutions and scripture can hold the key to the divine. We insult ourselves when we ignore the fact that the human being first emerged in Africa and ignore our debt to that continent and to those brave explorers who ventured into the unknown some hundred thousand years ago and began to traverse the globe, seeking new frontiers, new experiences, new ways of living.

We diminish all that we are and hinder all that we might be, when we refuse to see our humanity in the entirety of its history. We could not have evolved without all that happened before us. We carry evolution in our body, from the fourteen billion year old primordial hydrogen in our water, to the iron in our blood that was formed in the stars. We are *part* of this Universe. Life has brought us forth. Life is sustaining us.

Life in the form of bees who pollinate, trees who oxygenate, the oceanic phytoplankton who help to control the world's climate, each being playing their part in this interconnected and interdependent web. Our relatedness is basic to our existence, it is that which gives us life. The origin of all things from one source. How could it be any other way?

* * *

CREATIVITY AND IMAGINATION

There are times when it feels that the devastation being wrought on this planet is beyond repair, that we have done too much and gone too far. It can feel overwhelming and beyond hope. And then I remember that we live on a planet that is 4.6 billion years old and that we are part of a Universe that is currently 13.8 billion years old and that is still emerging. And this reminds me to trust again in the wisdom of these ancient, natural processes and more importantly, to try and learn from them so that my own behaviour becomes constructive and my actions are informed.

I have learned that fundamental to the nature of this Universe is creativity. This is a creativity that balances on a knife edge. In the initial unfurling of that fireball, science tells us that if the Universe had expanded one trillionth of a trillionth of a trillionth of a second faster, that the early matter would have spread apart too quickly and galaxies could not have formed; if it had happened one trillionth of a trillionth of a trillionth of a second slower everything would have collapsed back into a black hole as unrealised potential. Such elegance and precision. Even our own Earth, occupying as it does that slither of time/space that is the habitable zone, happens to be exactly the right size – a smaller planet may have burned out while a larger one might not have achieved the correct surface temperature for life to come forth – and the right distance from the sun, not too near so that we are burned and not so far that the rays of the sun are ineffective. Not only that, but our planet turns on an axis so that all sides receive the kiss of the sun. British Palaeontologist Richard Fortey wrote that *'if life is just a matter of chance, then the dice were loaded in its favour.'* And it would seem in this Universe that the dice are loaded in favour of something.

This creativity is such, that over and over in this Universe and on this Earth, the impossible has eventually become the inevitable. We can see such examples in the transformation from particles and atoms into swirling galaxies of stars; from dust into planetary systems, from seeds into lilies, from matter into consciousness. This Universe can bring into being from the narrowest possibility the most wondrously spectacular and intricate of formations, what would have seemed impossible appearing as naturally as if it were always here and just waiting to be unveiled.

From molten rock to oceans, continents, forests and jungles, the towering eucalyptus and the tiny, determined hummingbird, the noble, sauntering elephant and the bewildered and curious human being, creativity has fashioned a planet that in the words of Brian Swimme now 'sings opera'. A planet that exalts in diversity, a planet with the ability to respond to catastrophic situations with creative ingenuity. Consider this example: when the first cells over-ran their food supply they used their creative intelligence to capture the photon particle in flight and to convert its energy into the molecular structures for food, what we now call photosynthesis.

They did this without arms or brains or legs. This creative act was to be the foundation for the flourishing of life to come. We are totally dependent on the energy of the sun as is the entire Earth system. It courses through us, mobilising us, feeding us, warming us. The creativity inherent in the capture of its energy, the wildness of imagination that could dream up such a feat, is one example of the endless possibilities inherent in life. We live on a planet, in a Universe, with the capacity to constantly give birth to itself. The statement that there is nothing new under the sun reflects a mind-set whose eyes are closed because *everything under the sun is new*!

In tandem with creativity is imagination but what is the capacity of imagination, this thing that Einstein once said was greater than knowledge? In my view, it is the deeper modes of knowing, a response beyond rational thought, an activation of the hidden part of us where the Earth lives and dreams; it is the horizonless landscape of possibility and potential where what comes to us in vague, elusive dreaminess is etched into being. There are many ways to know the world. It is always coming to us, flooding us. It has been to our detriment that since the time of the Enlightenment we have valued science, rationalism and empirical modes of knowing over other modes of knowing such as the knowledge that comes to us through our senses, our feelings, our dreams and our intuition.

Right now, we have reached a point in the evolutionary history of the planet where the human being is creating its own evolutionary future. Until recently, the Universe evolved through its own processes, but now humanity is, ignorantly and destructively, altering those natural processes, so we are, to a certain degree, involved in how we will evolve. How we imagine the world is how the world will be. We imagined that life in Ireland would be better with a new motorway and so we created one, clearing woodlands and habitats and removing ecosystems that we depend upon. We imagined that society would be better without apartheid and so we worked to abolish it. We imagine that the world will be better without poverty and so we continuously work towards eradicating it. At the same time we imagine that life will be better if we are rich and so we orient our life towards earning and accumulation. Our imagination has the power to determine our reality. In our imagination lies the ability to form concepts and ideals of things that have never yet existed. The poet Rilke wrote *"fear not the strangeness you feel. The future must enter you long before it happens. Just wait for the birth for the hour of new clarity."* And this is our imagination, the future entering us and daring us to birth it. How marvellous it will be depends on our capacity to think beyond what we see in front of us, to think beyond the impossible, to be creative.

Passionist priest, Thomas Berry has written how the exterior shapes the interior. If we lived on the moon we would not have the environment necessary to create and shape our spirituality or evoke in us the wonder at the different manifestations and representations of beauty in the world. As it is, we live on a planet rich in colour and form and scent. To be able to wander free and let our mind be led by where this planet wants to take us next is the task of imagination; to forget ourselves and give ourselves over to the larger forces that permeate this world. And from this are such wonders produced as song and dance and language, religion, poetry and art; the first spacecraft, such acts as photosynthesis and respiration.

For too long we have lived locked into the narrowest of mindsets, thinking of our own individual lives as isolated and existing independently. We are pressured to conform to the cost of the unique quantum of creative energy that is our life and we reward such questionable behaviour as competition and professionalism. We look 'out' at nature and admire it forgetting that we ourselves have come from it and are as much 'nature' as the bird on the tree. It cannot be over-stated that the way in which we think as well as the values we hold, needs to be changed. There are many ways in which we could do this but just as the Universe can be thought of to be the primary revelation of the Divine, so too it can be thought of to be our primary teacher. Nature's ways are our ways, the qualities of the Universe are our qualities. Observing its principles and ways of being can only serve to guide our bewildered species as we seek a wisdom that as yet has eluded us. Imagination springs from hope and the promise of something to come, it is innate in each of us and will have no small hand in determining the human future.

* * *

Time

Our Universe is currently estimated to be 13.8 billion years old. It took roughly five hundred thousand years after its birth to create hydrogen, helium and lithium, the building blocks of creation. It took a further half a billion years for the first stars and galaxies to emerge and for the next few billion years there was continued star formation. It took roughly 10 billion years, after that initial flaring forth, for the Universe to arrive at the formation of Earth; ten billion years, over twice as old as Earth is now. After Earth was stabilised, it took approximately five hundred million years for the first cells to emerge, it then took a further two thousand million years for multi-cellular life to emerge.

The sizes of these numbers, to me, are meaningless and incomprehensible. But they do tell me three things. They tell me that the Universe that holds us is ancient. We are part of a body that predates the concept of time itself, which has existed for an impenetrable amount of time before our planet even came into existence, and which will continue to exist when our planet and all that it has created are but specks of dust in the rolling, spinning dark of space. The human being, on the other hand, is incredibly new. These numbers also reveal how it has been a slow, slow process which has filled the sky with galaxies and woven our Earth from dust and elements. Evolution takes a long time to occur. The third thing these numbers tell me, is that time cannot be fully understood by the way we measure it today, by the clock. In this story, time takes on another dimension. It ceases to be about days or months but begins to be about creativity and about what emerges, with each step building on the last.

Our Universe is time-developmental. It develops through time from simple to more complex forms, creating and recreating itself, transcending itself so that in some way it always becomes more than it was. What kind of intelligence is this? Energy becomes atoms, atoms become stars and a star explosion becomes the elements which make up Earth and every creature on Earth. Death driving life, destruction creating beauty, inextricably linked and each playing their part. And each creative act of our vast and astronomic past is present in some form now, has made 'now' possible so that the past is active in the present and creates the future, a chain of events seamlessly recreating.

Brian Swimme uses the analogy of the development of the Universe as being like a seed. He writes of how when a seed germinates, it initially focuses on bringing forth the roots. It is only when the roots are brought forth that it can begin to construct leaves, only when the leaves are brought forth that it can begin to construct flowers. Each step in its development is crucial, as a building block, and cannot be bypassed. And so it is with our Universe.

Not only does each event lay the foundation for what will happen next (be careful how you choose to act!), but every era of time is unique and every era of time can only occur when it is its time to occur. Brian Swimme gives the following examples. In the early Universe, you have the fireball and then you never have the fireball again. Similarly, when the hydrogen atoms emerged at the end of the fireball, it was time for the hydrogen atoms to emerge. They couldn't have been created any earlier because the heat of the fireball would have destroyed the atom. But when the time was right, hydrogen emerged and changed the nature of the Universe. Since that time, hydrogen has never been created again. Another example is the emergence of galaxies. Before the emergence of hydrogen and helium, the existence of a galaxy would also have been impossible but once they emerged and coalesced to form stars, the emergence of a galaxy became inevitable. We can say the same about Earth. The earlier stars could not have created planets as they were not developed enough to contain heavier elements, but the second generation stars did contain these elements and so gave us the materials needed to create our sun and solar system. We can also say the same about life. It could not have come forth until land and water were formed and the conditions were right for it. It was only created once but as a result the nature of the Universe as a whole was changed.

Time begins to mean something else when it is understood within the context of this great story. I repeat it is not about days or hours or the incessant ticking of the clock that binds us all to an energy that has been co-opted and divided by the captains of industry nor is it about any other diminishing division that people have devised. This Universe story shows us that time is about what emerges and what is created. The time for hydrogen, the time for Earth, the time for consciousness, the time for me. The Universe is an emergent process. It is not a place but a journey that is unfolding and that becomes more intimately engaged with itself through time. And each event is irreversible and non-repeatable. It cannot be repeated and it cannot be undone. As a particular manifestation of this Universe, I too, cannot be repeated nor can I be 'undone'. My once-off actions, my words and my thoughts will be knitted into and help to form whatever it is our future will eventually become. Doesn't this give us huge responsibility? Doesn't it make our lives and how we live them hugely important? Doesn't this change the nature of what it means to be alive?

I briefly had the privilege of studying and working on Genesis Farm with Miriam Therese McGillis. One of the things that Miriam taught there was the concept of Deep Time. The term was originally developed by Scottish geologist, James Hutton in the eighteenth century. Deep time is a geological understanding of time where history begins with the history of Earth 4.6 billion years ago and goes on to incorporate human history, as opposed to an understanding of time that begins with human history. It has now been extended to include the history of the Universe. Deep Time reveals how young we, the human being are, and aims to orient us into just how big the picture is, to expand our thinking so that we begin to see the larger trajectory of life and are aware of how many things have come before us and how our coming to be was so dependent on the events that preceded us. This is easier than it may first appear. Take the example of your own body. The water in your body contains primordial hydrogen that was created 13.8 billion years ago. The iron in your blood was created in stars that are at least 5 billion years old. All of time, all of evolution is carved into your body. Our bipedal physique was shaped by our environment, by our need to eat and be secure; our rotating shoulders by our arboreal ancestors; our freed arms and opposable thumbs so we could manipulate objects. And this is Deep Time – the acknowledgement of the seamlessness of creation, which links me and my body and my thoughts and behaviours to events that predate my species and even this planet.

Connected to Deep Time is the notion of Deep Vision. Because we more often than not, do not realise the age of Earth and how it brought us forth, we look at the world around us in a superficial and limited way. Quite simply, we do not see what is there before us. We have come, with grave and worrying result, to such a place in our understanding where we see trees as lumber, mountains as uranium, bogs as fuel sources without realising that they precede us and that they shaped us. Our planet has become a resource, not something to be communed with or to be intimate with or to learn from. We live in a mechanical and functional way and have slipped out of the sense of time as being about emergence, as coming through us. We have also slipped out of the conception of the Universe as having a sacred and spiritual dimension. Thomas Berry once wrote that the Universe is the primary revelation of the Divine, even before prophet and even before scripture. We have access to the Divine every time we draw a breath, every time we smell a flower, every time we chose to notice the depth of beauty that penetrates the world, fragile and mysterious, gently beseeching us to see and teasing us with its fleeting and intoxicating presence. It's in the light of the moon when it breaks through the night's clouds or the dew of a summer meadow when the day is only waking. It's in the song of the blackbird and the force of winter wind. It is everywhere there is life, everywhere there is laughter, everywhere there is breath. This Universe, the ultimate sacred body which continues to unfold even now. Perhaps poet Drew Dillinger encapsulates this notion most beautifully, when he writes "*the poet says' this entire travelling cosmos is the secret One slowly growing a body…*" A body that is becoming more complex, more differentiated, more beautiful and more alive… through time.

* * *

Death and Destruction

Our Universe did not emerge quietly or passively. The beginning as we know it, in so much as anything has a beginning, an explosion. It must have been loud and fierce, emitting light and particles, scattering its foetus across the darkness and violently becoming the space and time it was simultaneously creating – could that have been peaceful? Particles colliding and perishing, their existence bright, brief and then death. A spectacular unfolding, *the* most spectacular unfolding, equal parts beauty and creation, equal parts violence and destruction, not for human eyes but in it the seed from which human eyes would come. A fiery, busy, active beginning, already full, already fierce with determination and destined to create. In this beginning, we already see the many facets of our Universe.

We live in a Universe that is not only creative but is also violent and destructive. One of the most extreme examples of this is the Supernova explosion, when a star comes to the end of its life. It resists its death and burns all that it has within it to keep shining until it can resist no more and explodes outwards. As the star blasts apart sending its substance blazing through space, the heat and energy generated by this is the equivalent of a hundred billion stars. This supernova event is one of violent, burning intensity. With the death of the star however, new elements are created. In fact, it is only through the death of the star that these elements could be forged. Specifically, these are the elements necessary for the formation of Earth and for the origin of life. In the star's sacrificial destruction, something wondrous and further creative is born.

More locally, we witness destruction on our own planet in the form of storms, tsunamis, earthquakes, forest fires, volcanic eruptions, what the human calls natural disasters. These 'natural disasters' are the voice of a self-organising planet who strives to maintain its balance. It is easier for us to understand violence and destruction at a cosmic and planetary level than it is for us to understand it within ourselves. But this violent, destructive dimension is present at every level – elemental, organic, social and individual.

How does it happen that we build and detonate bombs, with no other intention than to kill and to destroy – burning villages, burning people, burning animals, burning houses until there is nothing left but the scorched and burning, bleeding, crying Earth? How does it happen that nations who are superficially divided by tribe or by religion turn on themselves and try to purge the country of all those who are different from themselves, to wipe them out entirely? Or that we hunt whale and elephant and dolphin to fuel the growing 'needs' of our consumerist world? Or that we dump toxic waste into our oceans killing thousands of life forms there as equally precious to this planet as we are? Or that we demolish the forests and pull apart the land, mine it, rape it, rob it so that we can wear gold watches and diamond earrings; poison the seas so that we can drive cars? I do not equate this destruction with the destruction that was at the beginning, it is not sacrificial because nothing is born of it. Its result is death but death without the promise of anything to come. A final, bloody and senseless death, an end in itself. Man-made. Why do we do it?

Thomas Berry writes that we have lost touch with the natural world at a very fundamental level. We no longer see ourselves as coming from and part of natural processes. We see ourselves as separate and independent of them. The natural world has become a backdrop to our existence, there only to facilitate the human, something we walk in and look at, not something that we are connected to and interwoven with. But this wasn't always our mindset. Diarmuid O'Murchu writes that humanity gets it right, not perfect, but right, for most of our time here on Earth when we remain close to nature. It is when we lose our place in the natural order of things, when we don't see ourselves as part but see ourselves as 'whole' that we act in deviant ways. He has written:

> *"...for most of our time here on earth, we behaved as an innovative, creative species. For most of that time, we got it right! As a creatively wise species we will always get it right rather than wrong, provided we remain close to the earth in which we are grounded and attuned to the cosmos to which we belong. Over the past eight thousand years of patriarchal domination we have not fared well. This has been one of our dark ages, and the massacre of 62 million civilians in the wars of the twentieth century amply verifies this. But eight thousand years is less than 1 percent of our entire story, and*

in all probability it is not the only time in which things went badly for humanity...will we forgive ourselves, outgrow this dysfunctional way of behaving, and opt to become a cosmic-planetary species once more?"

The human being is limited, anything that exists is limited. Our limits are set because as the universe unfolds so are we unfolding, incomplete, young, foolish and dizzy with all that we have been given, overwhelmed by the abundance of life and overwhelmed by our own powers and capabilities to manipulate it.

And manipulate it we have, we have made mistake after mistake trying to understand ourselves and the great cosmos that we are part of, trying to understand our role, the way that we should be, what we should do, trying to understand what it means to be alive and to walk on this Earth, trying to understand existence and afraid to at the same time.

And so terrified and overwhelmed by these thoughts we began to dominate, to try and have some control over the inevitable, to try to be 'in charge', to avoid being weak and vulnerable, mortal, insignificant. We made ourselves as Gods and began to rage and rage at the human condition and eventually at each other – unable to accept our limitations, unable to accept that we are not all-powerful, unable to accept our mortality, our finiteness, our humanness. But human is what we are and no matter how we try we cannot and will never be the beginning and the end. We will never be the total. We exist 'with' and 'because of', not as the cause.

One of the principles of the Universe which Brian

Swimme writes about, that has captured my imagination because in some way it speaks to these concepts of violence and destruction, is how the Universe is founded on Energy, Resistance and Dreams which could also be called Past, Present and Future. The dynamic of resistance indicates the privilege that it is to exist. All things resist and fight against the reduction of their presence in the world including the smallest particles. We feel inherently and innately our own value and contribution to this story. That is why day after day people choose to get up and live through the most 'dismal' circumstances. There is something innate in us where we feel the privilege of what it is to be part of this 13.8 billion year story. We feel the sacredness of it, the gift it is. It is this continued desire to exist that can contribute to the violence and the suffering that are part of this great adventure.

And what of death? This Universe story tells us how all beings, including galaxies, including stars, including Earth, have a life span. They are born, they live and they die. This remains one of the most difficult aspects of existence for humans to understand, that we are not eternal, that one day we will take our final breath and no longer be present to the world as we are now. No longer be able to feel water on our skin or to bend down and smell the reviving scent of the lily, no longer be able to hold a loved one close to us, feel the warmth of their breath, listen to their heartbeat. Our body will be inert and lifeless, matter without spirit and gradually matter without form.

To experience the death of someone we love and the grief and loss that accompanies it, remains too, one of the most painful aspects of existence. There is a finality to death that we struggle to understand, how something can be gone, never to be experienced again in the way in which we remember, in the way that is dear to us. But death is vital to life. It is the price we must pay for existence. In its darkness and sorrow, its bleak blanket of certitude, lies one of the truths of life, that life without death would not be life at all. Without death nothing new could emerge. There could be nothing new created. It would be a world that is the same, constantly, with no variation in beauty or sound or shape. A world without diversity, no new mornings, no new seasons, no new moments, no change. Death gives way to life. It enables life to continue. Life, not in the sense of my own individual life, but Life in the sense of this great Divine adventure started some 14 billion years ago. Life that continues to change and evolve becoming ever more beautiful and ever more differentiated and ever more sacred. Life that began in single celled organisms and developed into multi-cellular beings that in turn developed into reptile and mammal. Life that now sings and dances and plays. Life that now thinks. Life that now prays. If we revere life, then we must also revere death. One births the other.

* * *

Compassion and Justice

In death and destruction, we can witness how this Universe has a sacrificial element to its nature where the identity and individual self of something is given over for the greater life of the whole. We can see this in the death of stars for the creation of elements or in the extinction of dinosaurs for the flourishing of mammals, even at a more local level, in the death of the caterpillar to become the butterfly. This sacrificial element of the Universe is also contained in the life of the human. Death, suffering, loss, grief, hurt are as much part of our experience as we pass through the world in these bodies as is the sweet gift of life itself. And the human response to these is compassion.

Compassion is our ability to feel the pain of another beneath the inadequacy of their words and the changing expressions of their face, to intuit the depth of what they experience through the confused gulf that lies between two beings. It transcends language, race and species. We can know it because we also feel it. Life at every level includes loss in some form. It is the way of the world, a common thread that connects us and so our heart responds to the grief of another and seeks to console them drawing them close to us for comfort, placing our hand upon their hand, touching them because in some way the physical presence alleviates the spiritual loss and for some reason, loss is always more deeply felt in our spirit.

Matthew Fox writes *"compassion is about the actions that flow from us as a result of our interdependence."* Nobody can exist alone, we are each of us joined to and simultaneously part of the web that is life, entangled and intertwined with all the other creatures we share our breath with, with the air that sweeps across the globe, over the seas and mountains flowing in and out of each one of us; with the food that, nourished by the falling rains, grows up through the ground until we put it in our body; with the light from the sun that fuels the growth of the plant. Connected, in relationship, one living system. It is not strange then that we feel the suffering of another or that we seek to alleviate it drawing from us acts of beauty and hope and solidarity; it is not strange because as much as we are ourselves, we are also the Other and we seek to be whole. Compassion is the manifestation of our Oneness and it abides in the most brittle and bitter of hearts, the Divine touch softening the world with its gentle, healing presence.

As imagination is in tandem with creativity, so too is justice in tandem with compassion. When the Universe, or Earth, holds things in balance and equilibrium, justice is manifest on a grand scale. Here is an example – in the past four billion years, the sun's temperature has increased by 25%. Life will only survive if the surface temperature of Earth varies only very little. In response to the increase of temperature by the Sun, Earth adjusted the composition of its atmosphere to remain in that narrow, tight band which enables life to flourish. Life exists in balance and in order for this to be maintained there must be sacrifice. The darkening of the sky as the planet turns away from the sun, the bereft, bare trees of winter as Earth takes time to breathe. Sacrifice enables the maintenance of balance, facilitating the circle of reciprocity that each individual must partake in, a giving and receiving, life and death, never taking more than you need. It is right relationship and it is this quality that holds the Universe together. To be just at an individual level is to act from the knowledge that I am part of something that is greater than myself and to work on behalf of that. Life did not start with me nor will it end with me. Similarly, life did not start with the human and more than likely will not end with the human. We are a part, like so many other thousands of species who have come and gone, contributed and become extinct, we are not the whole. Justice is enabling this larger, universal venture, to continue.

* * *

Beneath the Surface
~ A Call to the Depths

The world is always coming to us. The sounds of the world through our ears. The sights of the world through our eyes. The tastes of the world through our mouth. The feel of the world through our touch and our body, flowing in and out of us as breath, as wind, as words, words that fill our head and mouth and are emptied again by our speech. It is a full world with so many billions of species, each individual striving to be warm and to be fed, clamouring to be heard, seeking out prey and hiding from predators, every one of us a manifestation of a Universe that is unimaginably vast, stretching out, mile after mile after black mile from us. We are encompassed by and encompassing, created by and creating, participant and spectator, so completely bound into and to this world.

In the commotion of life, we are often blinded by what we see and deafened by what we hear, but when we still ourselves, close our eyes and block our ears to all these externalities, we become aware of another current that flows consistently silent beneath this activity. This current seems to be deeper than the senses, somewhere that we cannot see or feel or touch but that comes to us in another way, making its presence felt by its effect. It resides in the darkness of the world, an opaqueness that is equally as effective as the sun and equally as active as the sea. It is the hidden dimension of the world, a presence beyond our senses. This presence invites us beneath the surface of things because life does not only happen on the outside, it also happens in the dark, in the underneath of things.

Two thirds of the surface of Earth is covered in water and we live and have our being on that one third that at present is not. It is here that our world is contained, it is here that we are most at home. We have built our homes and cities here, colonised its different landforms of deserts, mountains and forests. We live secure on this relatively thin crust, mostly unconcerned with the hot and flowing mantle it travels upon. The sea, we remain cautiously respectful of, knowing it holds its own wildness, a vigorous life force with the potential to rise up and envelope all around it – as it has done previously. We have travelled to the depths of this ocean, probed and analysed her and yet, there remains still, so much we do not know. In this everlasting sea, we get a glimpse of the depth of mystery that the world is built upon.

We know this about the sea, that it is much more vast and much more deep than our eye can drink in. We know this too when we raise our eyes to the heavenly splendour of twinkling stars, blinking in and out of existence, causing that dark space to seem benevolent and friendly – new human words for that which is ancient. And so too the world and what it is composed of, an energy that so little is known about, that is named 'dark' and that constitutes over 70% of what this Universe is. This hidden dimension permeates existence, an ever-present energy that is revealed through life itself, if we only take time to notice. If we begin to see the world as she takes her mighty breath and sends the kingfisher gliding through the sky, opens the petals of the rose, tumbles the rocks from the mountains, and scatters the sands in the desert. As she rises the tide ever higher and pulls it back into herself with rhythmic, deft grace, as she articulates herself in the speech of scholars and the play of children, this hidden dimension, a connection and current at the heart of all things, silent, alluring and generous.

Some four billion years ago, as the newly formed Earth was being pounded by rain, this hidden dimension was at work below the oceans in the churning, dynamic interior of Earth. The actions from within Earth causing volcanic unrest at the bottom of the oceans which in turn caused land to rise, pushing it to the surface. So too, did life begin to form beneath the surface, in the vents of rock under the sea, chemical gases combining and reacting, life without a membrane but life nonetheless. And what of the seed that we can plant ourselves, pushed deep into the damp and moist soil, covered and left in darkness. Who can understand the mystery that occurs when that seed some months later breaks through that soil, transformed in the darkness, perhaps by the darkness, into a tentative but vital bud.

Is it not the same thing repeated timelessly, surrender to the darkness, let yourself go deep into the unknown and that darkness and the alchemist power it holds will transform you. It is an act of trust. Of trust in the dark. Of trust in what we do not know and cannot see. Of trust that there is more to life than meets the eye. This is true for the seed as it is true for a child (are they not the same thing in any case?). The child takes shape hidden in the dark womb of her mother. All the formation that is needed, all the nutrients, the development of its little body, its arms and legs and organs, all happen in darkness, beneath the surface and hidden to the eye. It is real, we know it is real every time a baby is born, but that baby's conception, its growth, as the growth of the seed, as the churning interior of the Earth are all hidden dimensions to reality which take place beneath the surface. For some reason, they are not for us to gaze upon.

And high above us, above the clouds and the blue of our sky, encircling our planet in a magnetic field connected to the iron in the core of our Earth, and protecting us from the solar winds, is the magnetosphere. We cannot see it, perhaps for most people it does not even enter their consciousness but this protective shield lets in enough sun to light up our world and call the seeds from Earth but also prevents the intense solar winds from setting flame to our planet.

And what of our very own selves? Carl Jung once wrote of how there are as many galaxies within a person as there are that fill the Universe. We are that immense and so much of what we are and who we are happens also beneath the surface. All these things that the human being is made of – love, thought, forgiveness, anger, hatred, all these dimensions of reality that can only be known through their effect. And something is present where it has an effect.

Life is much greater than we can see. It is time to respect that and to be humble about our place and our knowledge. Alfred Schopenhauer said *"Every man takes the limits of his own field of vision for the limits of the world"* but the world is more deep than we can imagine, more full and layered than we can possibly know. Beneath the surface, under the exterior, in all that we cannot see or hear or touch, this is where the river runs that stirs us, this is where the mystery is, that divine spark of possibility and potential. This mystery that calls to be honoured, a sacred mystery that is slowly revealing itself.

*　*　*

AWE

I have a young niece who is new to being here. She walks through the day beaming like a sunflower at all there is to be explored and discovered. She delights in her existence and her existence is a celebration. She celebrates her taste by tasting everything, and her voice by singing when she pleases and as loud as she pleases, her touch by feeling what she passes sometimes gently but other times rough and squeezing. She imbibes life, takes it in through every sense. The smallest things captivate her. Her heart is open to the world, her mind free and at the same time enchanted, wanting to see all there is to see and to learn all there is to know. In her tiny frame and graceful presence, I see the nature of the human at its best.

She teaches me that we are made to marvel at life. As children, we do this naturally and unconsciously but time and lost dreams make us weary and cynical. And yet this ability to wonder at the world and to be in awe of our existence is part of who we are. It defines us. It is this that has propelled us to become the species that we are. It is this which will save us. From our earliest human form, the fact that we are alive, that we are here, has amazed us. Astounded by our voices, we learned to talk and sing, mesmerized by our arms and our legs, we began to dance. Enchanted by each other we fall in love and learn to make love face to face looking into the eye of the other with that sweet, fragile tenderness that only love can awaken in the human heart. The world is ours and we are the worlds.

The star still remains a source of amazement, the night sky and early dawn, even the distant, frozen moon. They move us to want to know more; the ambiguity of our own nature and how it both fascinates and compels us, also drives us to learn more and to want to be more. Our ability to wonder lies connected to the desire and the ability of the Universe to know itself. Our wonder and awe are transformed into curiosity and it is through curiosity that we learn about the world, that we have learned this story. The more we learn, the more we realize how deep into the history of the world we go, how entangled we are with every living system, how sacred the journey that the Universe has taken, how precious the gift of life. It is wonder, our ability to be astounded that will open us to this 14 billion year old adventure, that will allow us to be humble in the face of its unfolding, that will allow us to be generous in the receipt of its abundance, that will allow us to be loving in its bestowal of participation and that will allow us to be grateful in the observance of its mystery. This truly magical journey, more fantastical than any fairytale, more beautiful than any painting, the largest of mysteries and most sacred of prayers, in which right now, we are blessed to participate.

* * *

GLOSSARY

Amino acid: the component molecules of proteins.

Archaea: one of the three great domains of life, the others being bacteria and eukaryotes – the domain evolved from the first complex cell, which includes animals, plants and fungi. Archaea resemble bacteria but share many molecular similarities with eukaryotes.

Catalyst: a substance capable of speeding up chemical reactions.

Chloroplast: organelle (tiny organ) within the plant cell responsible for photosynthesis; originally derived from free-living cyanobacteria.

Cyanobacteria: an early type of bacteria, originator of photosynthesis.

Decoupling: the moment, 380 000 years after the Universe flared forth, when matter and light decoupled following the formation of the first hydrogen and helium atoms.

DNA: deoxyribonucleic acid, the molecule responsible for heredity.

Enzyme: a protein with the ability to speed up chemical reactions.

Hothouse: a period when it is too hot for ice to form at the poles; Earth has experienced Hothouse conditions for 85% of its history.

Hydrothermal vent: there are two types of hydrothermal vent. The first, the acidic black smoker, is well known. The second type is alkaline and rarer, arising when seawater chemically reacts with the mantle. Four billion years ago they were much more common, and their chemical and physical structure suggests they are a possible site for the origin of life.

Mitochondrion: organelle (tiny organ) within all complex cells, responsible for managing the proton electrical field and generating energy for the cell. Plural: Mitochondria.

Nucleic acid: essential molecular component of DNA.

Protein: a large and complex molecule, folded into a specific shape to undertake a specific task within the cell.

Proton electrical field: an electrical field created by differences in proton concentration on either side of the cell membrane.

Stromatolite: the first visible living structure, forming rocky reefs in shallow water; created by a symbiotic community of cyanobacteria and fermenting bacteria.

Supernova: an incredibly bright explosion of a massive star, in which all the heavier elements of the periodic table are formed.

* * *

Bibliography: Greg Morter

Armstrong, Karen (2006) A *Short History of Myth*. Canongate.

Berry, T. & Swimme, B (1992) *The Universe Story*. Harper Collins, N.Y.

Christian, David (2008) *Big History: The Big Bang, Life on Earth and the Rise of Humanity*. The Great Courses.

Dawkins, Richard (2004) *The Ancestor's Tale*. Phoenix, London.

Delsemme, Armand (1998) *Our Cosmic Origins: From the Big Bang to the Emergence of Life and Intelligence*. Cambridge.

Fortey, Richard (1997) *Life: An Unauthorised Biography*. Flamingo, London.

Frank, Adam (2011) *About Time*. Oneworld.

Gribben, John (2000) *Stardust: The Cosmic Recycling of Stars, Planets and People*. Penguin.

Helfand, David (2009) *The Physics of History*. The Great Courses.

Kors, Alan (1998) *The Birth of the Modern Mind: The Intellectual history of the 17th and 18th Centuries*. The Great Courses.

Lane, Nick (2002) *Oxygen: The Molecule that made the World*. Oxford

Lane, Nick (2005) *Power, Sex, Suicide: Mitochondria and the Meaning of Life*. Oxford.

Lane, Nick (2009) *Life Ascending: The Ten Great Inventions of Evolution.* Norton.

Martin, Anthony & Hawks, John (2010) *Major Transitions in Evolution.* The Great Courses.

Primack, Joel & Abrams, Nancy Ellen (2006) *The View from the Centre of the Universe.* Riverhead.

Roberts, Alice (2011) *Evolution: The Human Story.* Dorling Kindersley.

Roberts, Alice (2009) *The Incredible Human Journey.* BBC DVD.

Roberts, Alice (2011) *Origins of Us.* BBC DVD.

Sagan, Carl (1983) *Cosmos: The Story of Cosmic Evolution, Science and Civilisation.* Futura.

Swimme, Brian & Tucker, Mary Evelyn (2011) *Journey of the Universe.* Yale.

Tudge, Colin (2000) *The Variety of Life: A Survey and Celebration of all the Creatures that have Ever Lived.* Oxford.

Webpage: http://en.wikipedia.org/wiki/Chronology_of_the_universe.

Wilber, Ken (1981) *Up from Eden: A Transpersonal View of Human Evolution.* Quest.

* * *

Bibliography: Niamh Brennan

Berry, Thomas (1999) *The Great Work*. Bell Tower, N.Y.

Berry, Thomas (2009) *The Sacred Universe*. Columbia Press, N.Y.

Berry, Thomas (1988) *The Dream of the Earth*. Sierra Club Books, San Francisco.

Berry, T. & Swimme, B (1992) *The Universe Story*. Harper Collins, N.Y.

Conlon, J (2011) *Invisible Excursions*. Unpublished Manuscript.

Conlon, J (1994) *Earth Story, Sacred Story*. Twenty-third Publications, U.S.A.

Conlon, J. (2007) *From the Stars to the Streets*. Novalis, Canada.

De Chardin, Pierre Teilhard (1999) *The Human Phenomenon*. Appleton-Weber, S (ed.).

Lachman, G. (2010). Jean Gebser, *Cartographer of Consciousness*. EnlightenNext Magazine. Spring/Summer 2010.

Mahood, E. (2008) *The Primordial Leap and the Present: The Ever-Present Origin – An Overview of the Work of Jean Gebser*. www.gaiamind.org/Gebser.html.

O'Murchu, D. (2008) *Ancestral Grace, Meeting God in Our Human Story*. Orbis Books, N.Y.

Rainer Maria Rilke (2008) *Letters to a Young Poet*. BN Publishing.

Swimme, B.(1996) *The Hidden Heart of the Cosmos*. Orbis.

Swimme, Brian & Tucker, Mary Evelyn (2011) *Journey of the Universe*. Yale.

* * *

About the Authors

Greg Morter lives with his family and works as a gardener in Somerset. His fascination with the story of the Universe was kindled when he watched Brian Swimme's "Canticle to the Cosmos" in the early 1990s. Since 2009 he has been teaching the Universe Story in the form of a scaled walk in which each metre represents a million years in time. Further details can be found at **www.universewalk.co.uk**.

Niamh Brennan (MA International Development; MA Culture and Spirituality) is a writer and facilitator in Cosmology and Spirituality. Having studied under Brian Swimme and Jim Conlon, she is committed to the telling of the Universe Story and the implications it contains for our spirituality. Her latest book is *The human in the Universe* (Wyndham Hall Press, 2014).

* * *

GreenSpirit Book Series & Other Resources

We hope you have enjoyed reading this book, and that it has whetted your appetite to read more in this series and discover the many and varied ways in which green spirituality can be expressed in every single aspect of our lives and culture.

You may also wish to visit our website, which has a resources section, members area, information about GreenSpirit's annual events, book reviews and much more: **www.greenspirit.org.uk**

* * *

Other titles in the GreenSpirit book series

What is Green Spirituality?
Edited by Marian Van Eyk McCain

All Our Relations: GreenSpirit Connections with the More-than-Human World
Edited by Marian Van Eyk McCain

Rivers of Green Wisdom: Exploring Christian and Yogic Earth Centred Spirituality
Santoshan (Stephen Wollaston)

Pathways of Green Wisdom: Discovering Earth Centred Teachings in Spiritual and Religious Traditions
Edited by Santoshan (Stephen Wollaston)

Deep Green Living
Edited by Marian Van Eyk McCain

Free for members ebook editions

THE UNIVERSE STORY IN SCIENCE AND MYTH

GreenSpirit
magazine

GreenSpirit magazine, which is free for members, is published in both print and electronic form three times a year. Each issue includes essential topics connected with Earth-based spirituality. It honours Nature as a great teacher, celebrates the creativity and interrelatedness of all life and of the cosmos, affirms biodiversity and human differences, and honours the prophetic voice of artists.

Find out more at www.greenspirit.org.uk

"For many of us, it's the spirit running through that limitless span of green organisations and ideas that anchors all the work we do. And 'GreenSpirit' is an invaluable source of insight, information and inspiration."
~ JONATHON PORRITT.

GreenSpirit
Path to a New Consciousness
Edited by Marian Van Eyk McCain

Only by bringing our thinking back into balance with feeling, intuition and awareness and by grounding ourselves in a sense of the sacred in all things can we achieve a new level of consciousness.

Green spirituality is the key to a new, twenty-first century consciousness. And here is the most comprehensive book ever written on green spirituality.

Published by Earth Books
ISBN 978-1-84694-290-7
282 pages

Meditations with Thomas Berry
With additional material by Brian Swimme
Selected by June Raymond

Selected and arranged by June Raymond, especially for GreenSpirit Books, this is a collection of profound and inspiring quotations from one of the most important voices of our times, the late Thomas Berry, author, geologian, cultural historian and lover of the Earth.

Published by GreenSpirit
ISBN 978-0-9552157-4-2
111 pages

Printed in Great Britain
by Amazon